The Quotable Bible